WITH HIM IN THE STRUGGLE

Books in this series—

WITH HIM IN THE STRUGGLE

A Woman's Workshop on II Samuel

Myrna Alexander

Lamplighter Books Grand Rapids, Michigan

Zondervan Publishing House

This is a Lamplighter Book
Published by the Zondervan Publishing House
1415 Lake Drive, S.E., Grand Rapids, Michigan 49506

Library of Congress Cataloging in Publication Data

Alexander, Myrna.
  With Him in the struggle.

  "A Lamplighter book."
  1. Bible. O.T. Samuel, 2nd—Study. 2. Women—Religious life. I. Title
BS1325.5.A44   1986   222'.4406   86-5492
ISBN 0-310-37211-9

Edited by Pamela M. Hartung

Printed in the United States of America

86 87 88 89 90 91 92 93 / 10 9 8 7 6 5 4 3

To my Mother and Father
who created in their children
a desire to know God

CONTENTS

PREFACE

My eleven-year-old daughter, Christina, came bouncing into the room where I sat staring at a piece of paper entitled "Summary of Our Study in 1 and 2 Samuel."

"Can I get you to answer this new riddle from school?" she enthusiastically asked.

"Sure, but let me ask you a question, too."

To Christina's delight, I could offer only a funny, off-base response to her riddle. In contrast, she gave an insightful answer to my question.

"What does it mean to be 'after God's heart?'" I had asked.

She was silent for a moment and then quietly said, "It means loving God."

I was struck by her answer. She had said so simply what had taken me so long to begin to see.

"Well, what does it mean to love Him?" I pursued.

"It means reading His Word, talking to Him, and wanting to do what He says."

Wanting to continue our conversation, I quickly added, "What difference do you think it would make in a person's life if she loved God?"

"She would be happier," she said as she smiled.

"Why don't we do it then?" I responded.

"Because we think that we can make ourselves happy by getting what we want. And we think we're so busy that we don't have time to talk to Him and read His Word, so I guess it gets down to thinking we're just too busy to love God."

I sat there looking at her, wondering if she realized the significance of what she was saying and wondering, too, at God's working in both of our lives. Could it be, I marveled, that these past years of study in 1 and 2 Samuel had so affected my life that it was in turn affecting hers, too. Oh, how I prayed that it was true and that it would lead to her commitment to God and His ways.

The study in 1 Samuel, *After God's Heart,* brought us to the conclusion that to be after God's heart is to love God. The concept of love emphasized in the book is not one of lovely words but one of commitment. It is out of such a commitment to God and His Word that one obeys God. This commitment to walk in God's ways is seen as the only route to godly success.

In our present age of compromise and lack of commitment, we once again need to hear the call made in 1 and 2 Samuel to be a people after God's heart. (Note that this call was originally given during a period of history that was, in many ways, similar to our own.)

God has created us for a relationship with Himself, a relationship in which He loves us and we, in turn, love Him. In our day, however, we are usually too busy and too selfish to love God. If we care to do something about this sad situation, 2 Samuel is instructive for us. In 2 Samuel we discover real people who are in the process of struggling with how to love God in their everyday lives. King David in particular illustrates this struggle in his roles as leader, parent, and friend. Some of us will identify with David's responsibilities as a leader, but perhaps even more of us will identify with his struggles as a parent.

Reading 2 Samuel is like reading the morning newspaper. The issues frankly presented in this narrative are not only contemporary but also unpleasant. Reading 2 Samuel certainly will not give us "warm fuzzies," but it will give us instruction if we have ears to hear. Contemporary issues of incest, rape, adultery, murder, deception, pride, parental modeling, the results of not dealing with sin, and the over-indulgence of children are but a few of the subjects we will discover in this book.

"I found 2 Samuel to be realistic and instructive," my dear neighbor and friend said. "While I was studying this book, I was living out many of its pages in my own life!"

The practical relevancy of 2 Samuel is not always seen so readily. In fact, many people, on first reading 2 Samuel, miss its deep significance altogether. One Tuesday morning during our training time a woman spoke out in frustration. "I'm so disappointed and angry! After doing this week's lesson, I can't accept that David is known as a person 'after God's heart.'"

Though God's commentary on David said otherwise, this woman held firmly to her position. Her feelings were understandable because David fails and fails grossly! Yet does being after God's heart preclude failing?

Several weeks later the same young woman sensitively shared, "You know, I've always wanted to be a woman after God's heart, but that goal seemed so far away for me, so impossible to achieve. But now I have come to realize that David's life opens up the possibility for me to also be after God's heart. In fact, anyone who is willing to commit his or her heart to loving God, can become a person after God's heart!''

It is my earnest prayer that this study guide to 2 Samuel will enable all who use it to be motivated and enabled, within the struggles of life, to live after God's heart as these women are in the process of doing.

ACKNOWLEDGMENTS

For God's work to be done effectively, a variety of His people and their various gifts are needed. "To each one the manifestation of the Spirit is given for the common good" (1 Cor. 12:7). No work for God is achieved single-handedly, and no specific part is more valuable than another. Nothing is accomplished unless the necessary parts of Christ's body work together.

With Him in the Struggle illustrates well this principle because it is the result of God at work in His people.

I am thankful for the women in our weekly Women's Bible Study that originally studied this material on 2 Samuel. I am especially grateful for Doris, Lynn, Jan, Carolyn, Jeanie, Julie, Kay, Rosemary, Carol, and Olga, who were committed to meet every Tuesday morning for training and prayer in preparation for our Thursday Women's Study. Their interaction proved invaluable to me.

I am also grateful for the dedication, faithfulness, and skill of my typist and friend Julie Vawser, without whom these lessons would never have arrived at the publisher.

And once again, I am deeply grateful for my husband's encouragement and biblical counsel, as well as for the specific prayer support of my family, friends, and church family.

HOW TO USE THIS BIBLE STUDY

With Him in the Struggle was originally written for women who wanted to study the Bible together as a group after having studied a passage on their own during the week. I believe individual study is the key to a group Bible study whose goal is to see lives changed. Growth and encouragement took place in our group because we came together prepared to interact with God's principles.

Effective study of the Bible involves commitment. Consequently this study guide requires consistent and serious study. The result of the work is fruitful and life-changing group discussions.

The lessons are intended to be done on a regular basis: one discovery section per day, one lesson per week. There is, however, room for flexibility according to the needs of the individual or group using the material.

Finally, it is my prayer that each person who uses these studies will come to know the joy and growth that comes from daily studying God's Word.

SUGGESTIONS FOR LEADERS

The leader's primary goal is not to teach but to lead a discussion in which the participants feel free to share discoveries from their private study of the Bible. A wise leader can encourage learning by:

1. Trusting the Holy Spirit to work through her.

2. Providing a warm atmosphere in which all are encouraged to share.

3. Keeping the discussion "on track." The discussion should not be based on what people think but on what God's Word says. The lesson questions are designed to enable this. The leader can always ask, "How did you answer the next question?"

4. Attempting to cover all the assigned passages and questions. This encourages the participants to finish the study.

5. Maintaining this rule: Only those who have finished the week's assignment may share in the discussion. What better way to encourage study?

6. Shortening or rephrasing the questions, when necessary, for the sake of time or interest.

7. Varying the method. Some questions will lend themselves to discussion. At other times, an answer from one person may be sufficient. Sometimes observations from several women may broaden the group's understanding.

8. Summarizing the lesson. Some groups like the leader to summarize the lesson. A summary should give both the biblical principles found in the passages (see the "Key Principles" section at the end of each lesson) and the applications that specifically relate to the group's needs.

CYPRUS

• Aleppo

Euphrates River

Tiphsah •

Orontes River

Hamath •

• Arvad

Tadmor •

Great Sea

Gebal

• Lebo Hamath

PHOENICIANS

ARAMEANS OF DAMASCUS

Litani River

Sidon

• Damascus

DESERT

Tyre
+ Mt. Hermon
Kedesh • • Dan
Hazor ⊛ GESHUR

Acco •
• Kinnereth • Ashtaroth
Dor • Beth • Kenath
Megiddo ⊛ Shan Yarmuk River
GILEAD
Schechem • Jabbok River • Ramoth Gilead
SHARON
Aphek • Mahanaim
Joppa • Bethel
Gezer ⊛ Jordan River • Rabbah
Ashdod • ⊛ Jerusalem AMMON
Ashkelon • Beth Shemesh • Medeba
Gaza • Gath
PHILISTINES Ashan Hebron
⊛ Arad
Sharuhen Salt Sea
Beersheba • Kir Moab
MOAB

Baalath Beer Tamar • Zoar WILDERNESS OF JUDEA

Brook of Egypt

Kadesh Barnea
★ Hazar Addar

ARABAH

Bozrah

EDOM

Ezion Geber • • Elath

▨ Saul's kingdom, c. 1050–1010 B.C.
······· Israelite kingdom of David and Solomon,
c. 1010–930 B.C.
○ Solomon's major building projects
★ Fortified under Solomon

0   20   40   60   80 miles
0   40   80   120 km

THE EMPIRE OF
DAVID AND SOLOMON

1

THE GOD WHO IS WITH US

Overview and Introduction

When the slide-tape presentation *The Beauty of Holiness* ended, no one spoke, even though the large room of the retreat center was full. Each woman seemed to be in awe of the majesty and wonder of God portrayed on the screen.

Thinking of the young woman who was primarily responsible for the presentation, I thought, "Out of the ashes of her suffering has come this magnificent expression of praise to our God. Oh, Lord, only You could have given her this joy in place of sorrow."

Gloria's testimony of praise to her all-wise God was clear: "Lord, as I reflect on Your various 'training grounds' for me, I realize I could not be doing what I am now had it not been for what you have taken me through. Some of my experiences I termed 'bad'; others I called 'good.' Now I'm beginning to see that You allowed it all for good. You have taught me to know, 'As for God, his way is perfect' (Ps. 18:30)."

David, the shepherd boy who became the great king of Israel, made this same discovery several thousand years ago. Our study of 2 Samuel demonstrates God's faithfulness to carry out His Word. Many years before David was proclaimed king by his countrymen, God showed him that he would be the next king of Israel. David struggled to picture that promise actually taking place while he lived the life of an exiled fugitive, hunted as an outlaw by his countrymen. Yet as 2 Samuel begins, David the fugitive is anointed king over the house of Judah.

What takes us only a few weeks to study and meditate on in I and 2 Samuel consumed long hard years for David. Experiencing God's faithfulness at work in his life was, therefore, exceedingly wonderful to David.

In turn, this testimony of God's work in David's life should encourage and comfort us today. It is often hard to see God at work while we are enmeshed in the difficult circumstances of our lives. Sometimes it is only later that we can see His faithful hand guiding and protecting us through the struggles.

In the account of David's life recorded in 1 and 2 Samuel, we witness God at work in the seemingly confusing details of David's adventure. As we discover that none of David's training was wasted and no experience unnecessary, we are encouraged that the same is true for us today. The God who was with David wherever he went is the God who is with us today.

Cultural Insights

The training program that prepared David the shepherd boy to be David the king was successful. David was the strongest king Israel ever had. None of David's training experience was wasted when he was called to take a war-ravished and seemingly defeated nation and build an empire. Unlike King Saul, David's leadership of the country brought unification and development. David established a well-functioning government as well as a respected, organized priesthood, and a strong, successful army. When David became king, Israel was a disaster area that was struggling, disunified, and war torn. When David died, Israel was an efficient empire.

The fact that Israel was terribly disunified at Saul's death is demonstrated by the nation's split over who was to succeed Saul as king. David was quickly accepted by the people of Judah as king, but the tribes of the north crowned Ish-Bosheth, Saul's only surviving son, as their king. The tribes were still well aware of themselves as separate entities.

David did not rule the nation as a whole for seven and a half years. Yet without resorting to hatred, revenge, scheming, or plotting, David was soon recognized as king by all Israel. Saul's family was eliminated from political leadership when the one whom God had chosen to be king was finally crowned by the people. David would rule for thirty-three more years.

Undoubtedly David's time as an outlaw, as well as his residence with the economically superior Philistines, prepared him for military leadership. He had firsthand acquaintance with the formula and methods the Philistines used in the production of arms.

As Israel's enemies were subdued by her warrior king, the Lord expanded David's rule from the tribal area of Judah into a vast empire stretching from the river of Egypt to regions of the Euphrates. For the first time, Israel became the leading nation in the Fertile Crescent.

Jerusalem, the New Capital: David chose Jerusalem as the capital for a united Israel because of its strategic location. Jerusalem was in Judah, allowing David to be close to his loyal supporters in this tribe, yet it was located as far south as he could get and still be accepted by the northern tribes.

Jerusalem became the political capital of Israel when the army of men David had so carefully organized and trained during his time in exile turned to support him. When David brought the ark of the covenant to Jerusalem to be housed in a tabernacle, he restored proper worship on a national scale. Jerusalem thus became the religious as well as the political center for all of Israel (see 2 Sam. 6–7).

When David captured the Jebusite fortress, Zion became the "City of David," and Jerusalem "entered upon this historic career which has made it the most sacred and wonderful city of the world; a city, moreover, with a future even more wonderful than all its glorious and tragic past."[1]

DISCOVERY 1

1. Read chapters 1–4. List the victories David experiences. Record any insights that come to you as you read. _____

_____

_____

_____

_____

DISCOVERY 2

2. Read chapters 5–10. Continue your list of David's victories. Record any additional observations you make.

_____

_____

_____

_____

---

[1] J. Sidlow Baxter, Explore the Book, vol 2, Judges—Esther (Grand Rapids: Zondervan Publishing House, 1960), p. 70.

3. What three major promises does God make to David (2 Sam. 7:11–16)? _____

_____

_____

_____

4. What seven powers that surrounded the nation of Israel did David subdue (2 Sam. 8:12–14)? The map in the 1 Samuel study book *After God's Heart* or maps in your Bible will help you. _____

_____

_____

5. a. What does Scripture indicate was the key to David's triumphs over his enemies (2 Sam. 8:14)? _____

_____

b. How is this true in your own life? _____

_____

6. a. What was the secret to David's ability to unify the nation (2 Sam. 8:15)? _____

_____

b. In what spheres of your life will this secret be important for you to remember? _____

_____

_____

DISCOVERY 3

7. Read 2 Samuel 11–12. Record your insights. _____

_____

8. What mistake led to David's great temptation? _____

9. a. Summarize the temptation David succumbed to (2 Sam. 11:2–5). _____

b. How did David attempt to cover up his sin (2 Sam. 11:6–15)? _____

c. Why didn't David's cover-up scheme work (2 Sam. 11:26–12:1)? _____

d. How is this a warning to you? _____

10. How does this story apply to your own life? _____

11. What is significant about David's response to Nathan's confrontation? Why (2 Sam. 12:5–6)? _____

12. a. Psalm 51 records David's thoughts concerning his sin. As you read this Psalm, what four things impress you about David's attitude toward the events of 2 Samuel 11 and 12? _____

_____

_____

_____

_____

b. What do you learn about God in Psalm 51? _____

_____

_____

c. Which one of these truths about God encourages you most? Why? _____

_____

_____

DISCOVERY 4

13. Read 2 Samuel 13–18. List David's family problems.

_____

_____

_____

DISCOVERY 5

14. Read 2 Samuel 19–24. List the troubles David has with the nation. Record any additional insights. _____

_____

_____

_____

15. What do you think it means to be a person who has a heart after God? _____

_____

_____

2

WAITING FOR GOD'S TIMING

MEMORY VERSE: "I will instruct you and teach you in the way you should go; I will counsel you and watch over you" (Psalm 32:8).

It's difficult to wait on God when a hard situation is *almost* over, but not quite. When sticking to God's way means waiting, it's tempting to take things into our own hands. "I *can't* wait any longer! I *won't* wait!" our heart cries out.

David, too, could have said, "This is it! I have waited on God in my difficult circumstances for years. Now that those awful years of being hated, hunted, and forced to hide are over, I'm taking what is rightfully mine!" Now that Saul was dead, why shouldn't David go ahead and claim by force what rightfully belonged to him?

But the path to the throne was blurred as civil war broke out in the fragmented nation of Israel. The people of Judah made David their king, but the rest of the tribes stayed loyal to the house of Saul. To encourage this loyalty, Abner, Saul's nephew and the army's commander-in-chief, saw to it that Saul's son Ish-Bosheth was crowned king.

In spite of what may have seemed like a slow timetable, David accepted with an inner peace what God allowed in his life. David knew the character of his God and declared, "as for God, his way is perfect" (Ps. 18:30).

Cultural Insights

The Cities of Hebron: After Saul's death, God directed David to the cities of Hebron (2 Sam. 2:1). "Hebron" means brotherhood, and the group of cities known as Hebron served as the center of the confederation of families that made up Judah. Hebron, in the famous vineyard region about twenty miles south of Jerusalem, was the oldest city in the land. How appropriate that David should be crowned king in this old city in which Abraham, Isaac, Jacob, and Joseph were buried.

Polygamy: In David's time, political strength was increased through alliances that were sealed through marriage. Polygamy was the oriental way of establishing a royal house. Harems, therefore, were part of the court life. Though polygamy was the accepted custom in the nations around Israel, it seems God only tolerated polygamy in Old Testament times because of the hardness of Israel's heart. Polygamy always brought trouble to those involved (see I Samuel I, for example). Along with having many wives, kings commonly kept mistresses or concubines. To "lie with" a king's concubine constituted making oneself the king.

DISCOVERY 1/David, king of Judah

Read 2 Samuel 2:1—11

1. a. How did David determine what he should do after King Saul's death (2 Sam. 2:1)? _____

b. How is God's faithfulness to David demonstrated in 1 Samuel 2:1−4 (see also 2 Sam. 16:1−13)? _____

_____

_____

c. Are you unsure of how to respond to an issue in your life? What specifically have you done about it? In what way can 2 Samuel 2:1−4 encourage you? _____

_____

_____

_____

2. What does David's first act as king of Judah reveal about his character (2 Sam. 2:4−7)? _____

_____

3. a. Why do you think Abner wanted Ish-Bosheth as king and not David (2 Sam. 2:8−10; see also 2 Sam. 3:6−11)?

_____

_____

b. Think of circumstances in which this same situation occurs today. _____

_____

c. Convicted by his own words, what did Abner know about the one who was to be the next king of Israel (2 Sam. 3:9−10, 17−18)? If Abner already knew God's will, why do you think he had not responded to it before now? _____

_____

_____

_____

4. David knew that he had been anointed by God to rule over the whole nation (see 1 Sam. 16), yet he did not try to stop Saul's son from being crowned king. What does this indicate about David? _____

_____

DISCOVERY 2/Civil war begins in Israel

Read 2 Samuel 2 and 3.

5. a. Who initiated the terrible contest between King David's men and those of King Ish-Bosheth (2 Sam. 2:12–14)? (The expression, "Let the young men get up and fight hand to hand in front of us" refers to the ancient custom in which two enemy forces would agree to settle the issue by one battle.) _____

_____

b. What do you observe about the outcome of the day's sad events (2 Sam. 2:15–28)? _____

_____

_____

c. Briefly summarize 2 Samuel 2:17–32 as if you were a news reporter for the incident. _____

_____

_____

_____

_____

6. In what ways was this first battle prophetic (2 Sam. 3:1)?

_____

_____

7. a. What do you learn about God and His ways by comparing 1 Samuel 16:1, 12–13 with what happened fifteen years later in 2 Samuel 2–3? _____

_____

_____

b. In what way does this account encourage you today? Be specific. _____

_____

_____

DISCOVERY 3 & 4/The civil war ends

8. a. In 2 Samuel 3:2–5 the status of David's growing family is mentioned without commentary. According to Deuteronomy 17:15–18, what guidelines were given to the king of Israel? List God's reason (if stated) for a particular guideline.

_____

_____

_____

_____

b. What do these guidelines teach you about God? _____

_____

_____

c. What did David do about these guidelines (2 Sam. 3:2–5, 14)? _____

_____

9. Describe King Ish-Bosheth (2 Sam. 2:8–10; 3:7–11; 4:1). In who or what did Ish-Bosheth place his faith? What was the result of this choice? _____

_____

_____

_____

10. a. Though God anointed David to be king of Israel years before the event occurred, David *still* trusted God to carry out His plan in His way. As David waits on God, what significant event takes place in 2 Samuel 3:8–10, 17–19?

_____

_____

b. What can you do when you are tempted to take things into your own hands? _____

_____

11. Compare David's response to Abner (2 Sam. 3:20–23) with Joab's response (2 Sam. 3:22–30). What biblical principle did Joab break (see also Deut. 32:43; Rom. 12:19–21)? _____

_____

_____

12. Why did King David demand the response of 2 Samuel 3:31–37? Consider the result David's action had on the nation as a whole (see 2 Sam. 3:36–37). _____

_____

_____

13. What plan of action did David choose when he didn't know how to deal with the sons of Zeruiah (2 Sam. 3:38–39)? _____

_____

DISCOVERY 5/Ish-Bosheth's murder
Read 2 Samuel 4.

14. a. What were the motives behind the actions of Baanah and Rechab? _____

_____

_____

b. What did these men not know or remember about David (Compare 2 Sam. 1:1–16 with 2 Sam. 4)? _____

_____

_____

c. What principle from this chapter relates to being after God's heart? _____

_____

_____

d. How can you apply this principle to your life? _____

_____

_____

_____

* * *

Key Principles from Lesson 2

1. The first step in making plans is to ask the Lord (2 Sam. 2:1).

2. Waiting on God is not a waste of time (2 Sam. 1).

3. Take time to let others know you appreciate their good works (2 Sam. 2:1–7).

4. Do not rely on human ways to achieve God's goals (2 Sam. 2:8–11).

5. The warnings of Scripture are with purpose; ignoring them is dangerous (2 Sam. 3:2–5; Deut. 17:15–17).

6. Trust in God alone, not other people (2 Sam. 4:1).

7. God can cause someone who is against us to be for us (2 Sam. 3:9–10, 17–18).

8. Destroying others for personal gain is a sin and will be punished (2 Sam. 4).

3

GOD'S WAY IS EFFECTIVE

MEMORY VERSE: "As for God, his way is perfect; the word of the LORD is flawless. He is a shield for all who take refuge in him" (Psalm 18:30).

Waiting seems like a waste of time. We can hardly believe that God would allow, let alone plan such an activity. Yet how limited is our perspective! The Scripture declares the truth, "As for God, *his* way is perfect. . ." (Ps. 18:30, italics added). To those of us that are tired, frustrated, panicky, or angry about waiting, 2 Samuel brings hope.

Waiting on God is never a waste of time. Consider the useful effect the delay for David's coronation had on the nation. He was forced to wait on God during his time as the nation's outcast. Even after King Saul's death, it took another seven and a half years before all Israel saw David as the strong leader who could guide the nation out of the mess it had fallen into. Finally all the tribes sent large representations to David, begging him to become their king. David wisely took advantage of their enthusiasm and secured commitments from the people. David's wait had produced in the people a willingness to unify.

While the "elders of Israel" and David were signing a covenant in Hebron, a demonstration of unity and enthusiasm took place throughout the country. Thousands of radiant men from every tribe marched toward Hebron to declare David their king. Israel had never before known anything like this. Statistics in 1 Chronicles 12:24–37 account for approximately 339,600 warriors and 1,222 chiefs marching to Hebron. National unity and enthusiasm proceeded through a country torn by civil war. This acclaim is even more amazing when one pictures the scene of hundreds of thousands of men shouting allegiance to a man who had been the national outcast and fugitive. Now, as one body, the nation lines up behind David. God has so worked that David now becomes the unifier for the nation. God has been faithful to David.

During Saul's increasingly lax rule, David observed the need for unity among the greatly disunified tribes. Now David is in the enviable position of saying, in effect, "If you want me as king, here are the conditions." Though we do not know the specifics of the covenant that David and the people signed (2 Sam. 5:3), we can infer from what took place later, that the covenant must have included guarantees to secure a unified central government, organization, and taxation. God's way had not been slow; it had been effective.

David's attitude about the things of God is the opposite of Saul's! Saul ignored the ark, which was seemingly forgotten in Abinadab's home. David made transporting the ark to Jerusalem, as well as building a special place for it, one of his first tasks as king. When the ark was placed in the nation's political capital, godly worship was restored to the whole country. Where King Saul at one time murdered most of the priesthood, David humbly reverenced and respected the priests.

DISCOVERY 1/David, king of Israel

1. a. What did all the tribes of Israel finally realize about David (2 Sam. 5:1–3)? _____

_____

b. What does the people's declaration teach us about God (1 Sam. 16:1–13)? _____

_____

c. How does this encourage you? Be specific. _____

_____

_____

2. a. If David was about fifteen years old when the events of 1 Samuel 16 took place, how long did he have to wait to experience God's promise (2 Sam. 5:4–5)?_____

_____

b. What does this reveal about David? _____ _____

_____

c. Give an example of a time you waited to experience a particular promise from God. Explain the promise, your reactions, and the result. _____

_____

_____

_____

_____

DISCOVERY 2 & 3/Jerusalem becomes a governmental center (2 Sam. 5:6–16).

3. a. When the Jebusites said that the "lame and the blind could turn David away" from the city, they meant that

Jerusalem was invincible. What did David do, and what does this indicate about God (2 Sam. 5:6—9)? _____

_____

_____

b. Write down what you perceive to be an impossible situation in your life. Then write at least two things you have learned about God in 2 Samuel. _____

_____

_____

_____

c. What *new* conclusions do you have about your "impossibility"? _____

_____

4. a. According to 1 Chronicles 11:4—25 and 12:8—18, what type of men did the Lord gather around David to help him lead the nation? (List at least three characteristics.) _____

_____

_____

_____

b. Why were men with these characteristics especially helpful to David at this point in his life? _____

_____

c. What were the men like who came to David in the beginning (1 Sam. 22:1—2)? What may David have learned as he tried to lead this group? Why was this good preparation for leading a nation? _____

_____

5. What was David's secret to success? What can you learn from this (2 Sam. 5:10)? _____

6. Because of David's numerous leadership responsibilities, he didn't have time to develop "house-plans" for his home. In light of this, what great encouragement comes in 2 Samuel 5:11–12, and how does David interpret the event? What does such an interpretation reveal about David? _____

7. a. Consider David's actions in 2 Samuel 5:13 in the context of Deuteronomy 17:15–18. What do David's actions mean? _____

b. Think of an area in which believers today commonly break a specific command of God by following a culturally acceptable practice. In what area of your life may you be doing this? _____

8. a. How did David handle his first real crisis as king (2 Sam. 5:17–20)? What guidelines do you see here that can help you as you face difficulties this week? _____

b. Share one or more of these guidelines with someone (your child, a friend, etc.) this week and record the results. Be prepared to share these in your groups.

9. How did David view God's part in the Philistine battle (2 Sam. 5:20)? _____

_____

10. a. Summarize David's actions when the same problem arose again (2 Sam. 5:22–25). _____

_____

b. What qualities do you observe about David in his first two tests as king? _____

_____

_____

c. What do you learn about God from these events? _____

_____

_____

d. What personal significance does studying these experiences of King David have on your life? _____

_____

DISCOVERY 4 & 5/Jerusalem becomes Israel's religious center (2 Sam. 6).

As king, David tried to restore the ark of God to a place of prominence so that once again worship of the Lord could become the nation's central focus. David wanted to give the nation a religious center as well as a governmental one.

11. a. What appears to be the attitude of those bringing the ark to Jerusalem (2 Sam. 6:1–6)? _____

_____

b. Specific instructions about how to transport the ark had been given to Israel hundreds of years before in Numbers 4:4–15. As you compare these instructions with the account in 2 Samuel 6, what do you discover? What does this say about the people of David's time? _____

_____

_____

12. a. List David's reactions to the event that took place at the threshing floor of Nacon (2 Sam. 6:6–12). Why do you think David reacted as he did? _____

_____

_____

b. Through the seemingly confusing and unfair events of 2 Samuel 6, what was David forced to search out, consider, and learn (see 1 Chron. 15:1–2, 11–16, 25–28)? _____

_____

_____

_____

c. As you consider 2 Samuel 6:7 and 1 Chronicles 15:12–13, what crucial concept do you think God wanted His people to understand? What personal challenge is this to you? _____

_____

_____

d. When have you tried to do something for God but did not follow His way? _____

_____

_____

13. a. What was the attitude of David's wife Michal (2 Sam. 6:16)? Compare her reaction with the praise celebration of 2 Samuel 6:12–22. What may have been the basis for her attitude? _____

_____

_____

_____

b. We now observe the transformation of an attitude into an action. When David arrived home after a day of great joy, what kind of a reception did he get from Michal? Why? Describe David's response. _____

_____

_____

_____

c. Personalize God's message to you. _____

_____

_____

* * *

Key Principles from Lesson 3

1. God is faithful; He will do what He says (2 Sam. 5:1–5).

2. When God calls us to a task, He is faithful to perform the impossible (2 Sam. 5:6–12).

3. Knowing that the Lord God Almighty is with us is the basis for true greatness (2 Sam. 5:10).

4. In a time of crisis, take time to go to the Lord (2 Sam. 5:17–25).

5. Take time to get instructions from the Lord and then follow them (2 Sam. 5:17–25).

6. Reverence the Lord (2 Sam. 6:1–12).

7. When God gives us ways to pay reverence to Him, we should carry them out (2 Sam. 6).

4

GOD'S PLAN IS GREAT

Memory Verse: "How great you are, O Sovereign LORD! There is no one like you, and there is no God but you, as we have heard with our own ears" (2 Samuel 7:22).

*How can I give thanks for the things you have
        done for me?
Things so undeserved yet you gave to prove your
        love for me.
The voices of a million angels could not express
        my gratitude,
All that I am and ever hope to be, I owe it all to
        Thee.
To God be the glory . . . for the things He has
        done.*

> *MY TRIBUTE by Andraé Crouch[1]*

Have you ever felt like this—overwhelmed by God's unfolding plan for you? This song could summarize David's

---

response to God's plan for him revealed through the prophet Nathan. David, however, had not always been filled with wonder and awe for God's plan. During the difficult days recorded in 1 Samuel 27:1, David appeared to have lost hope. He thought, "One of these days I will be destroyed by the hand of Saul. The best thing I can do is to escape to the land of the Philistines."

What a contrast to see where God brings David in 2 Samuel 7. David is crowned king over the country from which he had been forced to flee. In chapter 7, God is in the process of revealing an amazing plan to David. His strategic message was most likely given to David at the height of his reign, when the successful wars listed in 2 Samuel 8 and 10 had made Israel the major nation in the Fertile Crescent and had made King David world-famous. (Note: the chronological sequence of 2 Samuel 6–10 was probably broken so that chapter 6 could tell the complete history of the religious movement under David.)

Although God's plan may have seemed unbelievable to David at the time, he was in the process of discovering that the events of his life would not only affect history but also stretch victoriously into eternity.

With humility and awe, David responded to God, "Who am I, O Sovereign LORD, and what is my family, that you have brought me this far? . . . How great you are, O Sovereign LORD! . . . Your words are trustworthy, and you have given this good promise to your servant" (2 Sam. 7:18, 22, 28).

It is possible that today you and I may not feel that God's sovereign plan for us is wonderful. We may be able to identify more with David's desert experiences (see 1 Sam. 19–30) than with his successes. Yet 2 Samuel 7 brings hope, for God's sovereign plan for David did not end in hopelessness in the desert but in a victory David will enjoy forever.

DISCOVERY 1/David's great desire

1. a. What comparison did David make between his own house and God's (2 Sam. 7:1–2)? _____

_____

b. David didn't just feel bad about this observation; he purposed to do something about it. What did David want to do, and why did he want to do it (2 Sam. 7:1–2; 1 Kings 8:17–18)? _____

_____

_____

c. According to 1 Kings 8:18–19, what did God think of the desire of David's heart? _____

_____

d. David sought to *do* something about his observations. Think of one specific thing you can do about a desire you have in your heart. _____

_____

2. a. When David shared his observations and conclusions with Nathan, what was the prophet's first response (2 Sam. 7:3)? _____

_____

b. In light of what follows in 2 Samuel 7:4–13, what do you conclude about Nathan's first reaction (see also Isa. 55:8–9)? What practical lesson do you draw from this situation, and how can you apply it to your life? _____

_____

_____

_____

3. In God's message to David through the prophet Nathan in 2 Samuel 7:4–16, who was going to build a "house"? What type of house was God talking about (state the verse references that support your answer)? _____

_____

_____

_____

DISCOVERY 2/God's covenant with David

4. a. Why was David denied the privilege of building the temple for God? Why was his son Solomon given the honor of building the temple (1 Chron. 22:6–10; 28:2–4; 1 Kings 5:3–5)? _____

_____

b. Describe a time when you were kept from doing something you thought was a good thing to do. _____ __

_____

_____

5. a. Using 2 Samuel 7:8–16 as your source, make a list of what God had already done for David. Then list what God states He *will do* for David. _____

_____

_____

_____

_____

_____

b. Why do you think God took the time to remind David of what He had done in the past? (It may be helpful to think why you also need reminders of what God has done for you.)

_____

_____

6. Years after the great promise of 2 Samuel 7:12−16 was given to David, many aspects of the promise were fulfilled. What promises made to David in 2 Samuel 7:12−16 were fulfilled in 1 Kings 8:2−21? What does this suggest to you about the rest of the promise? _____

_____

_____

_____

_____

DISCOVERY 3/The close relationship between Israel's king and her God

7. How long is David's house, throne, and kingdom to be continued (2 Sam. 7:16)? _____

_____

8. What type of relationship is going to exist between Israel's king and God (2 Samuel 7:14)? _____

_____

9. a. According to Psalm 89:30−32, what are David and his descendants *not* to do? _____

_____

_____

_____

b. What does God promise He will do if David's descendants sin in their role as ruler? What will God not do (2 Sam. 7:14–16; Ps. 89:30–37)? _____

_____

_____

_____

DISCOVERY 4/The eternal king of Israel

Part of the coronation process of Israel's king is the anointing by God's prophet. This anointing was important, for it demonstrated that the person who was anointed was God's choice and thus a true king of Israel. In Hebrew the word "Messiah" means "anointed one." In Greek the same concept is found in the word "Christ." Both terms are kingly words. The *eternal* king of Israel that was to come is referred to as *the* Messiah, or *the* Christ, both meaning *the* anointed one.

10. a. In light of the above, when the term "Messiah" or the term "Christ" is used with the name of Jesus, what does it mean? _____

_____

b. How is Jesus seen as the king of Israel, the Messiah, the Christ in the following passages?

Matt. 2:1–6 _____

Mark 14:60–65 _____

John 11:23–27 _____

John 12:12–16 _____

John 19:14–22 _____

11. In 2 Samuel 7:12–13 we learn that the eternal king of Israel will be a descendant (or son) of David. Jesus Christ's ancestral lines descend from David through Joseph (see Matt. 1:1–16) and Mary (see Luke 3:23–32). In 2 Samuel 7:14, we discover a father-son relationship between each king of Israel and God.

a. In Hebrews 1:1–8, to whom are the words of 2 Samuel 7:14 specifically applied? _____

_____

b. How was this close relationship demonstrated in Jesus' life in the following verses?

Luke 3:21–22 _____

Matt. 16:13–17 _____

Matt. 17:1–5 _____

John 10:24–30, 36 _____

John 12:49–50 _____

John 17:1–3 _____

c. In light of the above, what was the ongoing relationship between God and Israel's kings intended to picture?

_____

12. How has your understanding of Jesus as the Messiah, the Christ, grown as you studied these questions? What difference can this new understanding make in your life today? _____

_____

_____

_____

DISCOVERY 5/David responds to God

13. David's response to God's message is found in 2 Samuel 7:18–29. What does his response reveal about the characteristics of the person called by God, one after God's heart? Be sure to support your answer with verse references.

_____

_____

_____

_____

14. Even though David was not allowed to carry out his great plan, according to 1 Chronicles 22:1–5, what did he do? What does this say about his character? What personal application can you make? _____

_____

_____

_____

_____

15. a. Name two things you learn about God from 2 Samuel 7. _____

_____

_____

b. Which of these truths about God encourages you right now? _____

_____

* * *

Key Principles from Lesson 4

1. The things of God are top priority to the person who is after God's heart.

2. Our first impression of what sounds right or looks good may not be in agreement with God's will (2 Sam. 7:3–4, 12–13).

3. We must test our plans with God's revealed Word, not with feelings (2 Sam. 7:4–13).

4. God always has a reason for what He allows in our lives. God's ways are not our ways (1 Kings 5:3–4).

5. God's plans for us today touch tomorrow (2 Sam. 7:8–16).

6. We glorify God by how we respond to His will for our lives. We glorify Him when we:

a. focus on His character and respond in praise

b. accept His will

c. humbly submit to His will

d. thank Him for His ways

e. trust in His blessing (2 Sam. 7:18–29).

5

THE ALTERNATIVE TO HOPELESSNESS

MEMORY VERSE: "King David dedicated these articles to the LORD, as he had done with the silver and gold from all the nations he had subdued" (2 Samuel 8:11).

"And the LORD gave David victory wherever he went" (2 Sam. 8:6, 14). We tend to picture David moving through one victory after another in glorious succession with hardly a stubbed toe! Our lives, though, don't consist of a long line of successes. We experience times of real failure: failure to reach goals, failure as wives, failure as moms, failure as friends, and saddest of all, failure as God's friends.

In this lesson we look behind the scenes of 2 Samuel 8 and study David's own words in one of the Psalms he wrote during this period of conquest. We discover that David also experienced failure and hopelessness. In Psalm 60 we read of a situation that would have been hopeless to David had he not resolved to hope in the Lord his God.

Challenged by the truths found in this lesson, we discover another alternative to hopelessness. We can make a decision to hope in God.

Cultural Insights

David's kingdom: The expansion of David's kingdom into a vast empire stretching from the River Nile in Egypt to the Euphrates in Mesopotamia is only briefly recorded in the Bible. It is therefore all too easy not to realize how much time in each battle was devoted to hard work, inner struggle, inquiring, and waiting on the Lord.

One wonders about the untold stories that could elaborate on the special sufferings or joys that came as a result of the wars leading to the expansion of David's kingdom. "And David defeated the Philistines and subdued them . . . and David defeated Moab and measured them with the line . . . and David defeated Hadadezer . . ." and so on. Though brief in detail, 2 Samuel 8 is of great historic value for it records Israel's emergence at the beginning of the tenth century B.C. as the leading nation in the Fertile Crescent.

At the same time that 2 Samuel 8 outlines Israel's triumphs over her adversaries, it also indicates what had happened at home. Israel, under David's wise, God-inspired leadership, was finally unified. The jealousy, resentment, hatred, and bitterness that characterized the interaction between the tribes, making them an easy prey for their enemies, was set aside for a great goal: national unity. The separate tribes finally began to see that they had to be unified if they were ever to accomplish what God had called them to as a nation. Foreign war against adversaries cannot be fought without a strong home base.

This same fact also shows us something of David's strong leadership. Although the tribes evidently didn't appreciate it very much in the beginning, David forced the people to discover the joys of unity. This discovery was actually made possible through the policies and stipulations David negotiated with the people *before* he accepted kingship (see 2 Sam.

5:3). These policies were designed to guarantee true central government, and the tribes were forced to follow them if they wanted David as their king. Now, as Israel confronts its enemies, the tribes are able to stand together as one nation.

David's Army: The core of the army was most likely made up of the original 600 men from David's fugitive days. To this group was added a standing army of 288,000 trained men. This army operated on a monthly rotating system that involved 24,000 of them each month. However, all were ready for immediate action should the need arise. Finally, David provided for a group of foreign mercenaries composed of Cherithites and Pelethrites who formed a private bodyguard for the king.

It appears that David did not intentionally seek to go to war, but he simply took a stand when the need arose and tried to win. And David did win—continually. Thus Israel's borders expanded until all the land that was promised to Abraham's seed centuries before (Gen. 15:18) was under David's authority. Following the conquests, David's rule extended from the River of Egypt in the south to the Euphrates River in the north. In his day, David was probably the strongest ruler in the world.

DISCOVERY 1/David's triumphs

Read 2 Samuel 8.

1. Turn to the 2 Samuel map in this book or to the back of your Bible to a map of the Empire of David. Follow the conquests of David, referring to 2 Samuel 8. Which of these adversaries (the land areas are mostly under new names today) are currently a problem to Israel? _____

2. a. David ruled from the river of Egypt to the Euphrates in the north. To whom did God promise this land area centuries before (Genesis 15:18–21)? _____

_____

b. Reflecting on Genesis 15:18–21 and 2 Samuel 8, what do you learn about God that can affect your attitude about your circumstances? _____

_____

3. What reason does Scripture give for David's ability to accomplish great conquests (2 Sam. 8:6, 14)? What does this suggest to you personally? _____

_____

4. What helped unify the fragmented tribes of Israel (2 Sam. 8:15)? In what area of your life today can that same key be applied? State at least one specific way. _____

_____

_____

_____

5. What did David consistently do with the treasures that came from the conquests (2 Sam. 8:6–12)? _____

_____

DISCOVERY 2/David's thoughtful kindness
Read 2 Samuel 9.

6. At the height of David's power, when all the enemies of Israel had been defeated, what did David take time to do (2 Sam. 9:1–5)? Why (1 Sam. 20:12–17, 42)? _____

_____

_____

7. a. Why may Mephibosheth have experienced fear when he came before David (2 Sam. 9:6–7)? _____

_____

b. What did David do for Mephibosheth (2 Sam. 9:7–13)? _____

_____

_____

8. a. What qualities do the actions of David recorded in 2 Samuel 9 reveal to you? Why are these actions characteristic of one who loves God? _____

_____

b. Stop and ask the Lord to help you remember any important promise (made to your husband, child, or friend) that has not been kept. Ask the Lord to empower you to keep your promise in the best way. Be prepared to share with your group any action taken.

DISCOVERY 3/The great danger
In 2 Samuel 10 we get a closer look at one of David's conquests. It appears that the battle mentioned in 2 Samuel 8:3–6 was a major incident that occurred during the course of a great war against the Ammonites and their allies (2 Sam. 10–11). This great war was the major danger against David's kingdom.
Read 2 Samuel 10.

9. a. One can respond to kindness in two different ways. What kindness is shown in chapter 9? What is the response to this kindness? What resulted from it? _____

_____

_____

b. What kindness is shown in chapter 10, and to whom is it given? What is the response to the kindness? What resulted? _____

_____

_____

10. a. In the beginning of the battle recorded in 2 Samuel 10:6–12, what one word would have described the circumstances Israel faced? _____

_____

b. When Joab saw that the battle with the Ammonites and their allies was not going well, what did he do? Summarize 2 Samuel 10:9–15 in your own words. _____

_____

_____

_____

c. In spite of how things had looked at the beginning, what happened (2 Sam. 10:13–19)? _____

_____

d. What principle from this passage can you apply to your life? _____

_____

DISCOVERY 4 & 5/David determines to trust God

Read Psalm 60

The great war with the Ammonites was the major threat to David's kingdom. David wisely brought his awareness of the danger before the Lord. Though we often talk about our problems, we don't always bring our difficulties and dangers to the Lord in prayer as David did. Through the Psalms, we are allowed to see inside David as he faces the awesome task of battling a powerful enemy. From this man whose heart was after God we can learn principles that will help us cope with difficulties.

11. Why did David want to see his "house" remain forever? How is his reason different from that of many rulers today (2 Sam. 7:25–26)? _____

_____

_____

12. In contrast to the brief account in 2 Samuel 10, Psalm 60 gives the impression that this period of conquest was not easy for David. If it were not for Psalm 60, "we should have no inkling of the resilience of David's hostile neighbors at the peak of his power. His very success brought its dangers of alliances among his enemies (see 2 Sam. 8:5), and of battles far from home. At such a moment, when his main force was with him near the Euphrates (2 Sam. 8:3), Edom evidently took her chance to fall upon Judah from the south. The setting of the Psalm, then, is the deflating news of havoc at home (vv. 1–3), and of a defeat, apparently, at the first attempt to avenge it (v. 10)."[1]

As you read through Psalm 60, list some of the circumstances that David and his people experienced. _____

_____

_____

13. a. Psalm 60:3 makes clear that the outward crisis was matched by inward confusion and shock. Describe a time

---

[1] Derek Kidner, *Psalms 1–72* (Leicester, England: Inter-Varsity Press, 1973), 215.

when your circumstances did not appear to line up with what you knew was true about God. _____

_____

_____

b. David makes sense out of this chaotic time by tracing the hard things right back to God, seeing the entire situation under God's ultimate control. Name a situation in which you need to do the same. _____

_____

14. a. Summarize the prayer of faith found in Psalm 60:5 and 11, listing David's bold requests to God. _____

_____

_____

b. Summarize God's strong response to this prayer in Psalm 60:6–8. What does this suggest to you personally?

_____

_____

15. a. David humbly sees that the situation is beyond his own resources. According to Psalm 60:9–12, of what is David now keenly aware? _____

_____

b. What hope does David stand on in spite of the messages he has received from his circumstances?_____

_____

c. Stop and claim this same hope over your difficulties, even if the statements don't seem to apply to your present circumstances.

Key Principles from Lesson 5

1. We do not need to use human ways to be successful. We need the help of an all-powerful God (2 Sam. 8:6, 14).

2. Administration of a nation, a church, or a home with justice and righteousness promotes unity (2 Sam. 8:15).

3. A wise leader remembers to be kind. We are never too important to express thoughtful kindness (2 Sam. 9).

4. In spite of how bad circumstances look, God is always in control and will bring about His perfect plan (2 Sam. 10).

5. Therefore, when the circumstances are set against us, we cannot lose when we follow the Lord and His ways (2 Sam. 10:19).

6. We never waste time when we bring difficulties and fears of danger before the Lord (Ps. 60).

7. Apart from God, the help of other people is worthless (Ps. 60:11). With God, we will gain the victory (Ps. 60:12).

8. Our purpose in whatever we do is to glorify God's name (2 Sam. 7:26).

6

THE TURNING POINT

Memory Verse: "Then I acknowledged my sin to you and did not cover up my iniquity. I said, 'I will confess my transgressions to the Lord'—and you forgave the guilt of my sin" (Psalm 32:5).

King David is a powerful and important king. Israel's enemies have been conquered, one by one, as David experienced an unbroken series of military successes. In 2 Samuel 11 we see the Israelites take their final stand against the last enemy—the Ammonites. The military expedition against the Ammonite capital of Rabbah was so important that the Israelite army took the ark of God with them into battle. It appears, however, that David did not feel it was important for him to lead his army into this battle. He sent Joab in his place. This decision to compromise was significant for it led to the dramatic turning point in David's career.

Chapter 11 marks the pivotal point in our study of 2 Samuel. Chapters 1–10 set forth David's victories, but after chapter 11, chapters 12–24 emphasize King David's troubles. David had come close to the heart of God and through the Psalms had declared with great affection what God was like. David tramples under foot the intimacy he had known, and he sins against the Lord. Now we see him fall.

Unconsciously we cry out, "Oh no, David, not you!" How hard it is to watch this hero fall. Yet as Saint Augustine has said, "David's fall should put upon their guard all who have not fallen, and save from despair all those who have fallen."

May the earnest prayer from David's confession be answered in our lives. "Restore to me the joy of your salvation and grant me a willing spirit, to sustain me. Then I will teach transgressors your ways, and sinners will turn back to you" (Ps. 51:12–13).

DISCOVERY 1/David's sin

Read 2 Samuel 11.

1. What does 2 Samuel 11:1 imply about the character of David's leadership at this time? _____

_____

2. a. Show how the sin process discussed in James 1:14–15 is illustrated by 2 Samuel 11:2–5. _____

_____

_____

b. How has the process seen in James 1:14–15 recently been shown in your life? _____

_____

c. Becoming aware of our seemingly innocent first steps toward sin can keep us from falling again. Recall a time when you asked God to reveal to you where you first went wrong (or consistently go wrong) in a certain area. Of what did God make you aware? _____

_____

_____

3. a. Because of his initial sin, what further sin did David feel compelled to commit (2 Sam. 11:6–15)? _____

_____

b. Contrast David and Uriah. _____

_____

_____

_____

c. Why do you think David was irritated with Uriah's responses? _____

_____

_____

4. a. Continuing quickly in a tragic progression, David's previous sins now lead him to what drastic sin? Why do you think David felt the need to do this (2 Sam. 11:14–25)? _____

_____

b. From a human point of view, does it look as if David is "getting away" with his sin? Explain (2 Sam. 11:26–27). Of what was God aware as He saw David's actions (2 Sam. 11:27)? _____

_____

5. a. What two principles can you develop from 2 Samuel 11? _____

_____

_____

b. What two ways can you apply these principles to your life? _____

_____

_____

DISCOVERY 2/David's inner struggles over his sin

In the time lapse between David's sin and his confession, what went on inside of him? Once again the Psalms give insight into David's inner struggles.

6. a. What were the physical, mental, and emotional problems that developed in David after he sinned (see Psalms 32 and 38)?

David's Physical	Mental and Emotional Problems

b. How does it appear to you that David is "getting away" with his sin? _____

_____

7. What key does David give in Psalm 32:3 that reveals why miseries have come upon him? What does this say to you personally?_____

_____

_____

_____

_____

DISCOVERY 3/Nathan's rebuke

8. What did God do about David's sin and his resulting misery (2 Sam. 12:1)? _____

_____

9. a. How did Nathan get David to recognize his sin (2 Sam. 12:1–4)? Why was this approach a wise one? _____

_____

_____

_____

b. What point did God make to David in 2 Samuel 12:7–9? How should you apply this principle to your own life when you desire things that are contrary to God's Word?

_____

_____

_____

10. What did David despise, according to his actions (2 Sam. 12:9)? What does this suggest to you about your actions? _____

_____

_____

11. a. What did God say the consequences of David's sin would be (2 Sam. 12:10–12, 14)? _____

_____

_____

_____

b. Think of a modern example of a sin that makes "the enemies of the Lord show utter contempt" (2 Sam. 12:14).

_____

DISCOVERY 4/David's confession

12. a. What was David's response when Nathan confronted him about his sin (2 Sam. 12:13)? Is his response surprising to you? Why? _____

_____

_____

b. How is David's confession and God's response, through Nathan, an example of the New Testament truth stated in 1 John 1:9? _____

_____

_____

c. What application from this chapter can you make to your own life? _____

_____

13. God made a merciful declaration to David through Nathan in 2 Samuel 12:13. According to the Old Testament law of Leviticus 20:10, what could have happened to David at this point? _____

_____

14. a. What specific action about his problem did David take (Ps. 32:3–5)? What did he then encourage others to do (Ps. 32:6)? _____

_____

_____

b. What will result in your life if you respond to sin as David did in Psalm 32:5? (Make your list from Ps. 32:1–2, 5–8, 10–11.) _____

_____

_____

_____

_____

15. a. Describe the gift (or sacrifice) David desired to give to God as thanksgiving for what He had done for him (Ps. 51: 14–17). _____

_____

_____

_____

b. What changes would there be in your life if you had the attitude David expressed in Psalm 51? _____

_____

_____

16. What promise and warning does God give David in Psalm 32:8–9? Why was this good for David to know? _____

_____

_____

17. a. In what ways did David speak from experience in his two-part statement found in Psalm 32:10? _____

_____

b. What can you do when Psalm 32:1–10 is your experience (see also Ps. 32:11)? _____

_____

18. a. What is significant about David's response to his son's illness and consequent death (2 Sam. 12:14–23)? ____

_____

_____

b. After he confessed to the Lord, in what way was David able to be sensitive to Bathsheba during her time of difficulty? How did God encourage Bathsheba (2 Sam. 12:24–25)? _____

_____

_____

c. The name Solomon means peace. Why was this a significant name for David to choose for his son? _____

_____

19. In what ways are God's blessing restored to David (2 Sam. 12:24–30)? _____

_____

_____

* * *

Key Principles from Lesson 6

1. Irresponsibility to a task God has given us may make us vulnerable to temptation (2 Sam. 11:1).

2. Compromise with the Scripture weaves a thread that entraps (2 Sam. 3:2–5; 5:13–16).

3. Continual thinking about lust leads to sin (2 Sam. 11:2–5).

4. One sin leads to another unless confession occurs (2 Sam. 11).

5. We never get away with sin (2 Sam. 11:27; 12:1).

6. Not dealing with sin literally destroys us on the inside (Ps. 32:3).

7. When we sin, we sin against God (2 Sam. 12:9).

8. The person who is after God's heart does not rationalize sin but is straightforward: "I have sinned" (2 Sam. 12:13).

9. True repentance results in peace with God (1 John 1:9; 2 Sam. 12:13).

10. Sin has long-range consequences, even though God forgives and our relationship with Him is restored (2 Sam. 12:10–12, 14).

11. When we have peace with God, we are sensitive to the needs of others (2 Sam. 12:24–25).

12. When we have peace with God, we have joy in the Lord. Happy is the person who knows he or she is forgiven (Ps. 32:1, 11).

13. A broken and contrite heart is a holy gift to God (Ps. 51:14–17).

14. Unfailing love surrounds the person who trusts in the Lord (Ps. 32:10).

7

THE CONSEQUENCES AND THE WARNING

Memory Verse: "Create in me a pure heart, O God, and renew a steadfast spirit within me" (Psalm 51:10).

David could declare:

> How blessed is he whose transgressions are forgiven, whose sins are covered . . . I acknowledged my sin to you . . . and you forgave the guilt of my sin (Psalm 32:1, 5).

David could then pray in faith:

> Create in me a pure heart, O God, and renew a steadfast spirit within me" (Psalm 51:10).

Genuine repentance restores the joy of relationship with God, yet that does not mean that sin's scars are gone. Sin has consequences, and sometimes those consequences are permanent.

David was granted *forgiveness* by God for his sins of

adultery and murder, but the *consequences* of his sin were tragic. Not only was Uriah, David's faithful follower and supporter, dead, but David's own household was affected greatly. The effect of David's sin on his family and his kingdom demonstrates that sin is not a private matter that touches just the individual. During the twentieth year of David's reign, the consequences of his sin became visible when the selfishness of David's oldest son, Amnon, ushered in a long series of family and public troubles.

During all of these troubles, God never left David. When David called out to the Lord in humility, he experienced the comfort, guidance, and power of God.

In many ways this lesson may be hard for you, not because the lesson is difficult to understand, but because it is so sad. Though the events of 2 Samuel 13 and 14 took place more than three thousand years ago, it is as relevant to our day as the morning newspaper. As we approach these two chapters, 2 Timothy 3:16–17 is a challenge to us: "All Scripture is God-breathed, and is useful for teaching, rebuking, correction, and training in righteousness, so that the man of God may be thoroughly equipped for every good work."

DISCOVERY 1/Trouble in David's household

Absalom and Tamar were David's children by Maacah, the daughter of the king of Geshur (2 Sam. 3:3). Amnon was their step brother in that he was David's son by Ahinoam, the Jezreelitess (2 Sam. 3:2).

1. a. Read 2 Samuel 13:1–17. David's son Amnon had a problem with temptation. What does 2 Samuel 13:1–2 indicate he was doing about his temptation? _____

2. a. Read 2 Samuel 13:8–15. Did Amnon get what he wanted? Did it make him happy? Explain. _____

_____

_____

b. What was Amnon's attitude toward Tamar (2 Sam. 13:15–17)? _____

_____

3. a. Do you think Tamar was guilty or innocent in this incident? Why or why not? Support your answer from the passage (2 Sam. 13:8–14). _____

_____

_____

b. Summarize in your own words Tamar's response to her situation (2 Sam. 13:18–20). _____

_____

_____

4. What guidelines in this passage would help you resist temptations that you face? _____

_____

_____

DISCOVERY 2/David's response to Amnon's Injustice

5. a. What did David do about his son's immoral act (2 Sam. 13:21)? How do you view David's response in light of God's law revealed to Israel in Leviticus 20:17? _____

_____

_____

b. What way may David's response have influenced Absalom's future action seen in 2 Samuel 13:22–29? _____

6. What possible weakness does David reveal as he interacts with Absalom in 2 Samuel 13:24–27? _____

7. What practical application for your household is found in this lesson? _____

DISCOVERY 3/Absalom's response

8. Trace the progression of Absalom's response to the injustice done to his sister (2 Sam. 13:22–29). _____

9. What was Absalom actually doing when he decided to carry out the plan described in 2 Samuel 13:22–29 (Lev. 19:17–18; Heb. 10:30)? _____

What consequences did Absalom bring upon himself as a result of choosing his way and not God's (2 Sam. 13:37–39)? _____

DISCOVERY 4 & 5/David's response to Absalom's sin

Read 2 Samuel 14.

10. a. How did David handle his son's sin (2 Sam. 13:37–39; 2 Sam. 14:1–14)? _____

_____

_____

_____

11. a. What characterized David's behavior toward his son even after he allowed Absalom to return to Jerusalem (2 Sam. 14:23−29)? _____

_____

b. What resulted from David's way of handling Absalom's sin (2 Sam. 13:28−38; 2 Sam. 14:28−33)? _____

_____

c. Does it appear that Absalom ever repented of his sin? Does it appear that David applied the same principle at home that he used to rule the country (see 2 Sam. 8:15)?

_____

12. How did Absalom view himself? What may have encouraged him to have this view (see 2 Sam. 15:1−6)?

_____

13. Summarize several principles about the relationships seen in 2 Samuel 14. Apply one of these principles to your life. _____

_____

_____

_____

* * *

Key Principles from Lesson 7

1. Meditating on temptation hurts us (2 Sam. 13:2, 4).

2. Counsel must be evaluated in light of the Word of God (2 Sam. 13:5–7).

3. Giving in to temptation will not make us happy (2 Sam. 13:15).

4. When injustice falls under our jurisdiction, we must deal with it. If we are a parent, we must deal with our child's unjust acts (2 Sam. 8:15; 13–21).

5. Unjust people who are not made to see their errors feel justified in their acts (2 Sam. 15:1–6).

6. Lack of firmness encourages continued injustice (2 Sam. 13:24–29).

7. Avenging is the Lord's job, not ours (Heb. 10:30).

8. Forgiveness and acceptance go hand in hand. When we forgive, we accept (2 Sam. 14:21, 24, 32, 33).

8

THE BETRAYAL AND THE SUPPORT

Memory Verse: "My soul clings to you; your right hand upholds me" (Psalm 63:8).

No words properly describe the anguish of betrayal. Perhaps you have known the jabbing pain of betrayal in a marriage or friendship. For David the sorrow of betrayal came through his son's actions. The Book of 2 Samuel describes perhaps the most difficult time in David's life as he becomes aware of his son's desire to destroy him. In the midst of the disorientation and chaos, David cries out to God, "I stay close to you; your right hand upholds me" (Ps. 63:8).

David's testimony of divine support in the midst of heartache is a declaration of hope to us today. Though pain and sorrows plague us, the person who clings to the Lord Jesus Christ will find the sustaining comfort of God Almighty's right hand.

DISCOVERY 1/Conspiracy against David

In this lesson we continue to watch David experience something of the sorrow his disobedience and crime had caused his heavenly Father. David learns this pain through his own children.
Read 2 Samuel 15:1—12.

2. List Absalom's character traits (2 Sam. 13:19—29, 32, 37, 38; 2 Sam. 14:21—33). _____

_____

_____

_____

_____

3. How did Absalom try to turn the hearts of the people away from David (2 Sam. 15:1—6)? What similar appeals occur today? _____

_____

_____

_____

4. What disturbs you about Absalom's interaction with his father in 2 Samuel 15:7—10? Why? _____

_____

_____

5. What important role had Ahithophel played in David's life? How did that role change according to 2 Samuel 15:12, 31? What does this suggest to you? _____

_____

_____

_____

6. The conspiracy quickly grew to large proportions. What does this indicate (2 Sam. 15:12−13)? _____

_____

DISCOVERY 2/David's flight

7. In the midst of painful and shocking news, David makes a crucial decision. What is David's appraisal of his situation (2 Sam. 15:14)? _____

_____

8. Put yourself in David's place and consider what the officials' response would have meant to you (see 2 Sam. 15:15). Explain a situation in which you have made (or need to make) a statement similar to that of David's servants. _____

_____

_____

_____

9. Read and carefully observe the events of 2 Samuel 15:16−16:14, trying to imagine the emotions of such an hour. List your observations of the scene. Example: As David left this city, he was crying, his head was covered, and he didn't have any shoes on his feet (2 Sam. 15:30). _____

_____

_____

_____

10. Scripture records various reactions to David and his desperate situation. State the reactions of the following people as well as David's response to them.

a. David's servants (2 Sam. 15:14−15). _____

_____

b. Ittai, the Gittite (2 Sam. 15:18–22). _____

_____

c. Zadok and Abiathar, the priests (2 Sam. 15:24–29).

_____

d. Ahithophel (2 Sam. 15:12, 31). _____

_____

e. Hushai, the Arkite (2 Sam. 15:32–37). _____

_____

f. Ziba (2 Sam. 16:1–4; 19:24–30). _____

_____

g. Shimei (2 Sam. 16:5–8, 13). _____

_____

11. What distinction is made between David's two close counselors, Ahithophel and Hushai (2 Sam. 15:12, 37; 1 Chron. 27:33)? What does this distinction indicate to you?

_____

_____

12. a. What does David's response to his humiliating and desperate circumstances tell you about him (2 Sam. 15:13–16:12)? _____

_____

_____

_____

b. According to David's words, what did he have to offer those who stood by him (2 Sam. 15:19–20)? _____

_____

c. What attitude does David reveal in his response to Shimei (2 Sam. 16:5–12)? _____

_____

d. As you read through David's responses, what truth about God does David constantly acknowledge? _____

_____

_____

DISCOVERY 3/David's heart revealed

King David wrote some of the sweetest and most affirmative psalms during this sad time in his life. David reveals his heart and is an encouragement to future generations of believers.
Read Psalm 3.

13. a. Psalm 3 reveals some of David's thought processes as he flees from his son, Absalom. How is David able to face the devastating issue before him (Ps. 3:1–4)? _____

_____

_____

b. Because of David's confidence (Ps. 3:3–4), what is he able to do according to Psalm 3:5–6? _____

_____

_____

_____

c. Knowing his God, what could David say by faith (Ps. 3:7–8)? Put your answer in your own words. _____

_____

_____

   d. What truth about God encourages you from this Psalm? _____

_____

_____

_____

Discovery 4/David longs for God

Read Psalm 63, which David wrote when his circumstances forced him to live in the wilderness of Judah.

   14. a. At this point in his life, when David had seemingly lost everything, what does he need to satisfy himself (Ps. 63:1)? _____

_____

   b. What affirmation in Psalm 63:1 indicates why David could respond as he did to his circumstances? In what way do you identify with David here? _____

_____

   15. a. In Psalm 63, at what point does David mention his problem? Before this point, what would you say was his emphasis? _____

_____

_____

   b. What insight does this give you about your own prayer life? _____

_____

   c. According to Psalm 63:8, how is one preserved in the midst of difficulties? In light of this, what should you do to be sustained in the difficulties you are presently facing? _____

_____

_____

d. As you reflect on the circumstances David faced in 2 Samuel 15, how is his reference to himself as king in Psalm 63:9–11 a demonstration of faith? _____

_____

e. As you think about a difficulty in your life, write a statement that indicates your faith in God. _____

_____

_____

DISCOVERY 5/Absalom's two counselors

16. a. Absalom and his followers have triumphantly entered Jerusalem. Briefly summarize the counsel Ahithophel and Hushai give to Absalom (2 Sam. 16:20–17:14). _____

_____

_____

b. Which counsel did Absalom choose? Why? _____

_____

_____

c. All seemed lost for David, yet what does 2 Samuel 16:20–17:14 teach about God? Consider how you can apply this to your life and be prepared to share in your group. _____

_____

_____

_____

17. a. List ways God ministered to David's need in the midst of his suffering (2 Sam. 17:24–29). _____

_____

_____

_____

_____

b. Who in your life is a similar blessing? _____

_____

* * *

Key Principles from Lesson 8

1. We serve the Lord by following His Word. We cannot serve the Lord when we break a biblical principle. God's will is consistent with His Word (2 Sam. 15:7–8, 10).

2. Before concluding that we are right about something, we must evaluate it in the context of God's Word (2 Sam. 15:8, 10).

3. We need to support those who are in leadership (2 Sam. 15:14–37).

4. True loyalty counts the cost and decides "whether it means life or death, there will your servant be" (2 Sam. 15:21).

5. Loyalty means being willing to take risks (2 Sam. 15:32–37).

6. A trustworthy friend is consistent and does not change with the tide (2 Sam. 15:12, 32–34, 37).

7. In difficult circumstances, the path of wisdom is to realize that God is in control and to accept with a gentle, quiet spirit. One leads to the other (2 Sam. 16:10–12).

8. We can face difficult issues if we focus on specifics about God. Example: "But you are a shield around me, O Lord, my Glorious One, who lifts up my head" (Ps. 3:3).

9. God sustains us in difficulties. Therefore we can sleep peacefully and not be afraid of other people (Ps. 3:5—6).

10. It is God's job to bring salvation and blessing in our difficulties (Ps. 3:7—8).

11. Only a growing relationship with God satisfies our longings (Ps. 63:1—5).

12. In difficulties, we need to determine that God is our Lord and we will earnestly seek Him (Ps. 63:1).

13. In prayer, focusing on what God is like puts our problem in perspective.

14. Preservation in difficulties comes when we cling to God and discover that His right hand upholds us (Ps. 63:8).

15. No matter what the difficulty is, God is always in control and accomplishes His plan (2 Sam. 17:14).

16. God knows what we need and how to meet that need. He knows the perfect way to encourage us (2 Sam. 17:24—29).

9

HOW TO STAND WHEN YOU'VE BEEN FLATTENED

Memory Verse: On my bed I remember you; I think of you through the watches of the night. Because you are my help, I sing in the shadow of your wings" (Psalm 63:6—7).

There are times in life when we are shattered, times when we often feel helpless and don't know what to do next. As David left his beloved Jerusalem, he expressed such feelings to a group of supporters who sought to join him.

"Why should you come along with us? Go back and stay with King Absalom . . . You came only yesterday. And today shall I make you wander about with us, when I do not know where I am going?" (2 Sam. 15:19—20).

Today you may feel like a failure—as a friend, as a mother, as a wife. Perhaps your husband has chosen another woman over you, or maybe little is left of a ministry to which you have poured out your heart. Lurking in the corners of your mind may be that what's-the-use-anyway attitude that ends in hopelessness. What do you do about this attitude? How do you get up and stand once more when you're flat on the ground?

David was humiliated, weakened, and mocked. Yet in this lesson we see the result of David's decision to look away from the terrible circumstances in his life and shift his attention to God.

David used even the wakeful hours of the night to remind himself of what his God was like: "On my bed I remember you; I think of you through the watches of the night. Because you are my help, I sing in the shadow of your wings. . ." (Ps. 63:6–7). "But You are a shield around me, O Lord; You bestow glory on me and lift up my head . . . The Lord sustains me. I will not fear the tens of thousands. . ." (Ps. 3:3, 5–6) "Your love is better than life. . ." (Ps. 63:3).

Because of this perspective, David is able to declare by faith, "But the king will rejoice in God; all who swear by God's name will praise Him" (Ps. 63:11).

Cultural Insight

As you read through this lesson, you will find it helpful to note these cultural differences:

1. Riding a mule was a sign of royalty. For example, in 1 Kings 1:33 and 38, King David requests that his son Solomon ride on his mule. This action indicates Solomon as the successor to the throne. In this week's lesson, we read of Absalom riding into battle on a mule (2 Sam. 18:9).

2. In the ancient Near East, to "lie with" the king's wives and concubines was tantamount to usurping that king's throne.

DISCOVERY 1/The tragic battle

Read 2 Samuel 18.

1. a. In the midst of the chaos and heartache of the conspiracy, David took time both to focus on God and to get his situation into proper perspective (remember Psalms 3 and 63 in Lesson 8). How would you interpret David's actions in 2 Samuel 18:1–2? (The word "mustered" in 2 Sam. 18:1 also means "numbered" and "reviewed.") _____

_____

b. Compare the king's attitude in 2 Samuel 18:2 with that of 2 Samuel 11:1. What is the cause of the change in attitude? _____

_____

2. a. What conclusions do David's followers come to in 2 Samuel 18:3? _____

_____

b. Do you think their reasoning was wise? Why or why not? _____

_____

_____

c. What attitude does David display in his response to the people (2 Sam. 18:4)? _____

_____

3. a. What great concern does the king express as his followers depart for battle (2 Sam. 18:5)? _____

_____

b. What observation do you make as you compare David's concern here with his actions in 2 Samuel 14:24, 28, 30–32? What do you learn from this? _____

_____

4. a. The sovereign God allowed several factors to help David's small army as it faced the huge but hastily assembled troops under Absalom. Name at least two factors from the 2 Samuel 18:6–10 passage. ⸺⸺⸺⸺⸺

b. What can you learn about your own impossible situations from this passage? ⸺⸺⸺⸺

5. As you consider Joab's words and actions in 2 Samuel 18:10–16 and 19:1–7, what conclusions do you come to about his behavior? Be sure to give the verse references.

6. a. What were the consequences of the attempt to steal the throne from the God-appointed king of Israel (2 Sam. 18:9–17)? ⸺⸺⸺⸺

b. Contrast the monument of 2 Samuel 18:17 and that of 2 Samuel 18:18. ⸺⸺⸺⸺

DISCOVERY 2/The strange victory

7. What was Ahimaaz's great concern (2 Sam. 18:19–28)?

_____

_____

8. a. What seems to be the priority in the king's mind in 2 Samuel 18:29–33? _____

_____

b. What does David seem to miss in the news as a result of his sorrow (see 2 Sam. 18:28, 3l, 33)? Think of a time when you reacted as David did. Explain. _____

_____

_____

9. After carefully reading of 2 Samuel 19:1–5, list the actions that seem out of character for a victory celebration. What was the reason for such actions? _____

_____

_____

_____

_____

10. a. Would David's grief encourage his followers? Why or why not? _____

_____

_____

b. Using your own words, summarize Joab's challenge to David in 2 Samuel 19:5–7. _____

_____

_____

c. Are there times when it is best to put aside your emotions for the good of others? Explain. _____

_____

_____

DISCOVERY 3/David waits at Mahanaim

11. Summarize the practical dilemma the people of Israel faced in 2 Samuel 19:9–10. _____

_____

_____

12. What do you see David doing about Israel's dilemma (2 Sam. 19:11–14)? _____

_____

DISCOVERY 4/David at the Jordan

13. What two men needed to dread the king's return most? Why (2 Sam. 15:31; 16:1–13, 21–22)? _____

_____

14. What does David's interaction with Shimei indicate about the king's heart attitude (2 Sam. 19:15–23)? Did the king handle the situation with Shimei wisely or unwisely?

_____

_____

15. a. What is revealed when Mephibosheth meets the king (2 Sam. 19:24–30; 16:1–4)? _____

_____

_____

b. Describe the king's solution to the problem. Do you think his solution was wise? Why or why not? _____

_____

_____

_____

16. a. How did Barzillai support David in his adversity (2 Sam. 17:27–29; 19:31–32)? _____

_____

_____

_____

b. What were Barzillai's motives for helping David? Support your answer from Scripture. Think of a person in your life to whom you can be a Barzillai. Explain how you can do this. _____

_____

_____

_____

_____

17. What was the heart of the argument that took place on King David's return trip to Gilgal (2 Sam. 19:40–43)? _____

_____

DISCOVERY 5/Study observations

18. a. Reflect on 2 Samuel 18 and 19. Do you think David submitted to God's discipline (see also 2 Sam. 12:9–12)?

_____

b. What did the Lord do for David during his difficulties?

_____

_____

_____

19. In the midst of tragedy, where did David display a heart after God? Where did he not? _____

_____

_____

_____

*   *   *

Key Principles from Lesson 9

1. We must focus on God during our difficulties and see our situation from a biblical perspective. We will then be ready to take a stand (Ps. 3; Ps. 63; 2 Sam. 18:1–2).

2. Because God is sovereign and all-powerful, He can accomplish His purposes with a few people as well as with many (2 Sam. 18:6–10).

3. Never try to do yourself what God alone can do (2 Sam. 15:10; 18:9–17).

4. When we are obsessed by a certain thing, we often miss what God has done (2 Sam. 18:28–32).

5. At times we may need to put aside our own sorrows for the good of others (2 Sam. 19:5–7).

9. We cannot build a monument to ourselves. God builds the monument (2 Sam. 18:17–18).

10. When we don't understand God's priorities, we may be tempted to vie for positions of importance (2 Sam. 19:41–43).

10

"OH NO, NOT A NEW PROBLEM!"

Memory Verse: He said: "The LORD is my rock, my fortress and my deliverer; my God is my Rock, in whom I take refuge, my shield and the horn of my salvation. He is my stronghold, my refuge and my savior—from violent men you save me" (2 Samuel 22:2–3).

"Oh no, not something else! Oh, not now!" You've just come through a hard time, and you're struggling to get your bearings. You think it's time for a breather between crises. But here you are facing a new storm.

"I just can't handle another difficulty right now!" you exclaim. Most likely David felt the same way as he crossed the Jordan River to be reinstated as the king of Israel after one of the hardest times of his life. Suddenly, David was in the middle of a new crisis that had the potential of doing ". . . more harm than Absalom" (2 Sam. 20:6). "All the men of Israel withdrew from following David and followed Sheba" (2 Sam. 20:2).

The Psalms of David written during this difficult period indicate his focus and resulting reliance upon the Lord. They give us encouragement and direction when we feel, "This time, I've had it!"

DISCOVERY 1/David faces a new difficulty

Read 2 Samuel 19:41–43 and 2 Samuel 20:1–7.

1. a. What confronted David in the midst of his victorious return to Jerusalem (2 Sam. 19:41–43; 20:1–2)? If you had been in David's position, what emotions would you have experienced? _____

_____

_____

b. How does Scripture describe Sheba (2 Sam. 20:1)? What exactly did Sheba do (2 Sam. 20:1–2, 7, 14)? _____

_____

_____

c. What word or phrase would you use to describe the actions of the men of Israel (2 Sam. 20:2)? _____

_____

2. a. What did David do about this difficulty (2 Sam. 20:4–6)? _____

_____

_____

b. Why didn't Amasa lead David's troops against Sheba as initially planned (2 Sam. 20:4–6)? _____

_____

c. What was David's priority in dealing with the rebellion (2 Sam. 20:4–6)? Do you think this was wise? Why or why not? _____

_____

_____

3. a. How did David "set his house in order" when he returned to Jerusalem (2 Sam. 20:3)? _____

_____

b. Consider: "Life in a king's harem carried with it the possibility of dire consequences as well as the reward of luxurious living." What were some of the consequences David's ten concubines experienced (2 Sam. 16:21–22; 20:3)? _____

_____

_____

4. List your insights from this passage. _____

_____

_____

_____

DISCOVERY 2/The encounter

Read 2 Samuel 20:8–13.

5. a. What do Joab's actions toward his cousin Amasa indicate about his character (2 Sam. 20:7–10; see also 2 Sam. 19:11–13)? _____

_____

_____

b. What was the people's first reaction to Joab's action (2 Sam. 20:11–13)? What happened when the "problem" was removed from sight? _____

_____

_____

DISCOVERY 3/Destruction is averted

Read 2 Samuel 20:14–26.

6. What began to happen to Abel Beth Macaah once Sheba arrived (2 Sam. 20:14–15)? _____

_____

_____

7. Who averted the destruction of the city? How (2 Sam. 20:16–22)? How is this person repeatedly described? What does this suggest to you? _____

_____

_____

_____

_____

DISCOVERY 4/The famine

With the conclusion of 2 Samuel 20, the last uprising against David ends, and with it the political history of David's reign.

It appears that the five subjects treated in the concluding chapters of 2 Samuel are not a continuation of the book's narrative ending in 2 Samuel 20. It is impossible, therefore, to know the time of the famine discussed in 2 Samuel 21:1–14.

8. a. Read 2 Samuel 21:1–14. When a major difficulty affected those for whom David was responsible, what did he do (2 Sam. 21:1)? _____

_____

b. Think of a situation in which you need to do as David did. _____

_____

9. What reason does God give to David for the hardship that is occurring in his life (2 Sam. 21:1–2)? _____

_____

10. a. Compare Israel's judgment with the commitment their forefathers had made years before (Josh. 9:1–27, especially vv. 18–21). _____

_____

b. What did God's people neglect to do before making the original commitment (Josh. 9:14–16)? _____

_____

c. In spite of their forefathers' error, were the children of Israel still committed to keeping the promise their forefathers had made? Explain (Josh. 9:15–20). What was to happen to Israel if they weren't faithful to the commitment (Josh. 9:20)? What took place years later to reinstate this commitment (2 Sam. 21:2, 5–6)? _____

_____

_____

_____

_____

11. a. Develop some principles about commitment, using 2 Samuel 21:1–3 and Joshua 9:1–27 as your guide. _____

_____

_____

_____

b. In light of the above: 1) as a wife, what specific applications can you make? 2) as a mother, what specific things should be part of your children's training? 3) as a single woman, what specific applications can you make?

_____

_____

_____

_____

DISCOVERY 5/David responds to God's purpose

12. a. After David discovers the cause of the famine, what specific actions did he take (2 Sam. 21:2–9)? _____

_____

b. State in your own words the priority issue that is at stake (2 Sam. 21:3; Josh. 9:19). _____

_____

c. How are David's actions faithful to this priority? To what other commitment is David also being faithful (2 Sam. 21:7; see also 2 Sam. 9:1, 7; 1 Sam. 20:12–17)? _____

_____

e. Make a personal application from this passage. _____

_____

_____

13. In spite of what David had to do as king of Israel, how did he show compassion toward the sorrow of Rizpah (2 Sam. 21:8—14)? _____

_____

_____

* * *

Key Principles from Lesson 10

1. Every difficulty in your life should be entrusted to God in order for proper action to result (2 Sam. 20:1—6).

2. A woman who supports her actions and attitudes with Scripture is wise (2 Sam. 20:16—22).

3. When those we are responsible for are in trouble, we should seek the Lord on their behalf (2 Sam. 21:1).

4. Always seek the Lord before making a serious commitment (Josh. 9:14—16).

5. God expects us to keep our commitments (Josh. 9:16—20).

6. We witness for or against God, depending on how we keep our commitments (Josh. 9:19; 2 Sam. 21:1—2).

7. It is wise to model for our children our faithfulness to commitments.

11

SONG OF THANKSGIVING

Memory Verse: "You are my lamp, O LORD; the LORD turns my darkness into light. As for God, his way is perfect; the word of the LORD is flawless. He is a shield for all who take refuge in him" (2 Samuel 22:29, 31; see also Psalm 18:29–30).

David typically concluded his military enterprises with a grateful review of all that God had done in the campaign. David needed to take time to acknowledge in detail God's goodness and faithfulness. Unlike many of us who move through one difficulty after another, never pausing to declare God's wonderful deliverance, David was as careful to thank God for mercies, past and present, as to ask Him for future needs.

The Psalms are filled with David's songs of thanksgiving. But in 2 Samuel 22, we find David's grand hallelujah. In this psalm David, the warrior king, reflects on what God has done in his life. David thanks God for the deliverances and good gifts of the past and then expresses unbounded confidence in God's mercy and goodness for the times to come.

David specifically praises God for His commands, which bring victory. At one point in the psalm, David claims that the successes he experienced were not because of his own abilities, but the successes resulted from having followed his heavenly Father's instructions.

The heroic exploits of David's men are also found in the concluding chapters of 2 Samuel. May this review of heroic acts and unbelievable feats summon us to realize the Lord's power within the impossibilities of our own lives.

DISCOVERY 1/Heroic exploits

Read 2 Samuel 21:15–22. Note that we do not know the specific time period of the events in 2 Samuel 21–23.

1. What does 2 Samuel 21:15–22 indicate about the type of men who served David? _____

_____

_____

2. Think through the truth set forth in 2 Timothy 3:16–17, and then suggest several possible reasons why 2 Samuel 21:15–22 has been included in God's Word. _____

_____

_____

DISCOVERY 2/David's declaration of God

3. As you think about God today, take time to reflect on David's great declaration about God in 2 Samuel 22.

a. What strong pictures does David give us of God in 2 Samuel 22:2–3? _____

b. Summarize the concept David shows us in 2 Samuel 22:2–3. ⸏⸏⸏⸏⸏⸏⸏⸏⸏⸏⸏⸏⸏⸏⸏⸏⸏⸏

c. How can these verses encourage you this week? Be specific. ⸏⸏⸏⸏⸏⸏⸏⸏⸏⸏⸏⸏⸏⸏⸏⸏⸏⸏⸏⸏⸏

4. a. What types of difficulties does David state he often faced (2 Sam. 22:5–6, 17–19)? ⸏⸏⸏⸏⸏⸏⸏⸏

b. Based on what David knows (and takes time to consider) about God, what does he do in trouble (2 Sam. 22:2–7)? What is your first response in times of difficulty?

DISCOVERY 3/God responds to David

5. a. Briefly summarize God's response to David's cry for help (2 Sam. 22:7–17). ⸏⸏⸏⸏⸏⸏⸏⸏⸏⸏⸏⸏

b. What does this picture suggest to you about God's interest in His children? What does it suggest to you about your role as a parent? _____

_____

_____

6. a. What testimony does David give about his need and God's action (2 Sam. 22:17−21)? _____

_____

_____

b. Since our God is "the same yesterday, today, and forever" (Heb. 13:8), what meaning does 2 Samuel 22:17−21 have for you in light of your present needs? _____

_____

_____

c. Describe a time in which you were aware of the Lord's mighty working on your behalf (see Col. 1:13−14 for other examples). _____

_____

_____

_____

DISCOVERY 4/The possibility of blamelessness

7. a. What is David now able to say about his actions and attitudes toward Saul (2 Sam. 22:21−25 along with the wise warnings found in 1 Sam. 25:23−31, especially vv. 26, 28, 30−31)? _____

_____

_____

b. Can you ever say of yourself what David says in 2 Samuel 22:22–24? How does this challenge you? _____

_____

_____

DISCOVERY 5/What God does for David

8. a. When David didn't know what to do in a situation, what did he remember (2 Sam. 22:29, 31)? _____

_____

b. What challenge do these verses give you for this week? _____

_____

c. How does 2 Samuel 22:31–32 assure you when you wonder, "Is God's way right in this situation?" _____

_____

d. What does God become to you when you make a decision to take refuge in Him (2 Sam. 22:31)? In what area of your life do you need to make this decision right now?

_____

_____

9. a. Make a list of all that God has done for David, using his testimony in 2 Samuel 22:33–49 as your guide. _____

_____

_____

_____

_____

_____

_____

_____

_____

b. Which of these actions encourage you as you realize God can do the same in your life? _____

_____

_____

_____

10. a. Because of all God has done for David, what does David say he will do (2 Sam. 22:50)? _____

_____

b. It is interesting to note that Paul makes this same declaration in the New Testament to show that Jews and Gentiles would be involved together in what great action (Rom. 15:8–11)? _____

_____

c. Apply this to your own life. _____

_____

11. a. What decision (like the one David made) does 1 Peter 4:19 encourage you to make today? _____

_____

b. In what ways does the psalm found in 2 Samuel 22 illustrate the wisdom of making such a decision? _____

_____

_____

c. How can sharing this truth with your children help them in their present situations? _____

_____

12. a. Discover five or more principles in David's song of praise for how you should live your life. _____

_____

_____

_____

_____

_____

b. Take two of these principles and show how you applied (or can apply) them to your life this week. _____

_____

_____

13. Take time today to look back over the ways the Lord has delivered you. List some of them here. _____

_____

_____

_____

*　*　*

Key Principles from Lesson 11

1. We praise the Lord with thanksgiving when we specifically declare what He has done for us (2 Sam. 22).

2. We need to remind ourselves continually of what our God is like (2 Sam. 22:2–3). Then we will be encouraged to call upon God in faith (2 Sam. 22:4–7). For example, David reminded himself during difficulties that God was a rock, a fortress, a deliverer, a refuge, a stronghold, a shield (2 Sam. 22:2–3).

3. God responds to His children's cries for help (2 Sam. 22:7–17)..

4. God's actions are directed to our specific point of need (2 Sam. 22:17–21).

5. As we appeal to God, we must also review our actions and attitudes (2 Sam. 22:22–24).

6. In any situation, coming to God lights our way (2 Sam. 22:29–31). When we question if what happened was right, remember: God's way is blameless; His word tested. We are "shielded" from evil when we make the decision to take refuge in God (2 Sam. 22:31–32).

7. When we first realize who God is and what He has done for us, and then remind ourselves of these truths, we will be motivated and encouraged to "commit ourselves to our faithful Creator and continue to do good" (1 Pet. 4:19).

12

A MORNING WITHOUT CLOUDS

Memory Verse: "Therefore I will praise You, O LORD, among the nations; I will sing praises to your name" *(2 Samuel 22:50).*

It had been raining day after day. And now again it was raining as I sat at my desk studying David's last public words to his people. While I was studying, I was also struggling to accept a heartache in my life. Pensively I read those words spoken so long ago: "he [and his rule] is like the light of morning at sunrise on a cloudless morning, like the brightness after rain that brings the grass from the earth" (2 Sam. 23:4).

These were lovely words and a beautiful picture, yet somehow that day I could only see the rain.

The next morning as I awoke, I didn't hear the familiar sound of the rain. Walking outside, I was overwhelmed by the brilliance of the sunshine, the clearness of the sky. How fresh and new everything looked in the sunshine after the rain. Suddenly the words that I had pondered the day before began to make sense to me. This is what the rule of God is like in my life! When I'm submissive to His rule, the result is like the joyous beauty of this morning. Quietly, I submitted my heartache to His rule.

In this week's lesson, David's last words prophesy a glorious, future hope. I hope these words will be as relevant to you as they were to me.

DISCOVERY 1 & 2/David's last words

1. How does David view himself at the close of his life? What observations do you make here (2 Sam. 23:1)? _____

_____

_____

2. a. As we read David's last message, who are we to recognize as the speaker (2 Sam. 23:2–3)? _____

_____

b. How then, should you view these last words of David? _____

_____

c. What further insight do you get as you compare David's statement with that of the apostle Peter's in 2 Peter 1:21? _____

_____

3. a. According to God, what two qualities are necessary for godly leadership (2 Sam. 23:3)? _____

_____

_____

b. What is such leadership like (2 Sam. 23:4)? _____

_____

_____

c. As you consider the pictures God gives in 2 Samuel 23:4, what results can godly leadership produce in your life?

_____

d. How can you relate these two aspects of godly leadership to any leadership positions you have (as a mother, as a head of a committee, as a teacher, etc.)? _____

_____

_____

4. To what ruler do David's words ultimately refer, according to Isaiah 11:1–5 and John 1:1–5, 14? What has been your own response to this ruler? _____

_____

_____

5. What covenant (agreement) had God previously made with David (2 Sam. 23:5; see also 2 Sam. 7:12, 16; Psalm 89:34–37)? How is this covenant described? _____

_____

_____

6. a. Why do you think this covenant is mentioned again? (Consider *who* is speaking, *when* he is speaking, and the *emphasis* of the message.) _____

_____

_____

b. What does David's assurance (2 Sam. 23:5) that God would keep His covenant indicate about his knowledge of God? _____

_____

c. How can people today become a part of this same covenant? _____

_____

d. In light of these verses, have *you* become a part of this covenant? Explain. _____

_____

7. **a.** What promise for the future is made in David's message (2 Sam. 23:3–5)? _____

_____

b. What warning is given (2 Sam. 23:6–7; see also Matt. 13:39–43)? _____

_____

8. **a.** When God includes a list in His Word, it is with purpose. Why do you think God included the information found in this passage (2 Sam. 23:8–39)? _____

_____

_____

b. As you reflect on this list, what other observations do you make? _____

_____

_____

_____

DISCOVERY 3/The sinful command

Though we don't know chronologically where to place the following important event, it doubtless took place late in David's reign. It was not, however, at the very close of his rule, even though it comes at the end of 2 Samuel. The kind

of census described in this passage is one which a king would probably make during his years of strength.
Read 2 Samuel 24.

9. a. How is the Lord described in 2 Samuel 24:1? The verse begins, "Again. . . ." This also happened in 2 Samuel 21: 1–2. What do you think is the root reason for this reaction? _____

_____

_____

b. According to 1 Chronicles 21:1, who was the unseen instigator of this event? _____

_____

c. What human being was used to effect evil (2 Sam. 24:1–2; 1 Chron. 21:1–2)? _____

_____

10. a. What command did David give in 2 Samuel 24:2?

_____

b. From 2 Samuel 24:1–13, determine:

1) Who first saw the command as sinful? _____

2) Who next judged the command as sinful? _____

' 3) Finally, it was seen as sinful by whom? _____

11. a. In light of Joab's response to David (2 Sam. 24:3), what did David think would bring happiness? _____

_____

b. What may have come into David's heart, allowing him to want to take a census? _____

_____

c. What did Joab try to do about this situation? _____

_____

d. Instead of giving David delight or pleasure, how did his actions affect him (2 Sam. 24:10, 12–17)? In light of this, do you think Joab was right in trying to stop David? Why or why not? _____

_____

_____

e. What application do you see here for your own life?

_____

_____

f. According to David himself in Psalm 30:6, what may have been the reason for David to think that he would "not be shaken." (Notice also that both the 2 Samuel 24 and 1 Chronicles 21 account of this event are preceded by a list of military heroes.) _____

_____

DISCOVERY 4/Sin's effect

12. a. What was David's clue that something was wrong (2 Sam. 24:10)? _____

_____

b. What did David do about this clue? _____

_____

c. Instead of this response, what other responses often are made in situations similar to the one described in 2 Samuel 24:10? _____

_____

d. After a night of confession, what did David encounter in the morning (2 Sam. 24:11–13)? _____

_____

_____

_____

e. What practical warning do you observe? _____

_____

13. In light of 2 Samuel 24:14, what was David's reason for selecting the third judgment from the Lord? Do you think this was a wise conclusion? Why or why not? _____

_____

_____

14. a. In what ways do the statements of the prophet Gad to David (2 Sam. 24:13), as well as what took place in 2 Samuel 24:15, demonstrate that sin affects others? _____

_____

b. Since numbers were so important to David, what may God have been trying to show him and the nation through this judgment? _____

_____

c. What lesson or principle do you draw from this passage? _____

_____

DISCOVERY 5/The plague is stopped

15. a. What were David and Israel's elders doing while God's judgment fell on the nation (1 Chron. 21:14–16)?

_____

_____

b. Express in your own words David's prayer (2 Sam. 24:17; 1 Chron. 21:17). _____

_____

_____

c. What characteristic revealed in David's prayer would you like to see in your own life? _____

_____

16. a. Even before David's prayer, what had God's mercy already moved Him to do (2 Sam. 24:16)? _____

_____

b. Even so, what was God's response to David's prayer (2 Sam. 24:18; 1 Chron. 21:18)? _____

_____

c. What was David's immediate action when God's Word was set before him (2 Sam. 24:18–20)? _____

_____

17. a. In what ways does God go before and prepare Araunah's heart (1 Chron. 21:18–23)? _____

_____

b. How can this help you when God calls you to a particular task? _____

_____

18. a. Describe David's attitude about his offerings to the Lord (2 Sam. 24:22–24). _____

_____

   b. What strong contrast to David's attitude is given in Malachi 1:11–14? _____

_____

_____

   c. What has been your own attitude about your "offerings" to the Lord? _____

_____

_____

19. a. State the divine response that came as David offered his sacrifice before the Lord (2 Sam. 24:25; 1 Chron. 21:26–28). How was the fire of the sacrifice kindled? _____

_____

_____

   b. What future importance was this place of mercy to have (2 Chron. 3:1)? _____

_____

20. a. What did David conclude when God appeared above the threshing floor (1 Chron. 21:26–22:1)? _____

_____

   b. In light of David's great desire expressed in 2 Samuel 7:2, why may this have been a time of particular joy to David? How did David express his joy (1 Chron. 22:2–5)?

_____

_____

21. What kind of temple did David foresee? What was David's heart motive for such a magnificent temple (1 Chron. 22:5)? _____

_____

_____

* * *

Key Principles from Lesson 12

1. We gain a healthy self-image when we view ourselves as God views us (2 Sam. 23:1).

2. When we read God's Word, we realize that the living God is speaking directly to us (2 Sam. 23:2–3).

3. According to God, the two aspects of godly leadership are righteousness and reverence for God (2 Sam. 23:3).

4. Responding to godly leadership will bring peace, freshness, and light into our lives (2 Sam. 23:4).

5. The Righteous Ruler is Jesus Christ (Rev. 19:11–16).

6. God will always be faithful to His promises in His Word (2 Sam. 23:5–6; Ps. 89:3–4).

7. Sin makes God angry (2 Sam. 24:1 with 2 Sam. 21:1–2).

8. When we choose not to walk in God's ways, we open ourselves up to being used by Satan to effect evil (2 Sam. 24).

9. We need to take a stand against sin. To do so we must help each other (2 Sam. 24:3).

10. To take a proper stand against sin, we must know God's Word (2 Sam. 24:3).

11. We need to be sensitive to God's warnings. We must listen when others question our actions in light of the Word (2 Sam. 24:13), and we must not ignore a troubled conscience (2 Sam. 24:10).

12. We cannot take sin lightly; sin has consequences (2 Sam. 24:11–15).

13. The wise are humble before God (1 Chron. 21:14–16).

14. Even when we know God is going to punish us, it is wise to cast ourselves on His mercy (2 Sam. 24:14).

15. When God calls us to a work, He prepares a way for the task to be accomplished. If this involves others, He prepares their hearts (1 Chron. 21:18–23).

16. Because the Lord is the great King, we should offer Him the best (2 Sam. 24:24; Mal. 1:13–14).

17. God's temple shows what God is like (1 Chron. 22:5).

13

THE CHARGE

*Memory Verse: "Observe what the L*ORD *your God requires: Walk in his ways, and keep his decrees and commands, his laws and requirements, as written in the Law of Moses, so that you may prosper in all you do and wherever you go" (1 Kings 2:3).*

The words "To our children, David, Christina, and Jonathan who we pray will desire to be after God's heart" are written on the dedication page of *After God's Heart*, the study book about I Samuel. The purpose of those words was not to look nice on the page, but to convey to our beloved children a message of greatest importance.

The Scripture declares, "The eyes of the Lord range throughout the earth to strengthen those whose hearts are fully committed to Him" (2 Chron. 16:9). We want His eyes to see that our children's hearts are His. We want them to know His strong support in their lives.

Therefore, communicating the priority of knowing God and following in His ways is the most important thing we can do for them. And when this priority becomes their hearts' desire, then they will be after His heart.

My husband and I are not perfect at this job. We have had many good intentions that have seemed to fail, and there have been times our own sin has gotten in the way of accurately communicating what knowing God and following in His ways involves.

But God is powerful. Through the strength and wisdom of His Spirit we have had opportunity to demonstrate to our children in many practical ways the same important reality of David's charge to his son: "Observe what the Lord your God requires: Walk in his ways, and keep his decrees and commands, his laws and requirements, as written in the Law of Moses, so that you may prosper in all you do and wherever you go" (1 Kings 2:3). David wanted Solomon to succeed, and he knew that the only route was to follow God's ways. Before Solomon could follow God's ways, he had to know them. David, therefore, stressed the priority of God's Word to his son.

David teaches us a practical lesson through his challenge to Solomon. When we respond to David's message, our children witness the good effect of God's truth in our lives. In turn they will be encouraged to live life God's way.

DISCOVERY 1/The final crisis in David's life

Read ' 1 Kings 1.

1. Cultural Note on 1 Kings 1:1-4: Medical science in David's time held that warmth was brought to the aged by the body of another human being. That the body heat had to be from a young and beautiful human being was no doubt an extra, even in David's culture.

2. a. Even in his old age, David faced problems within his household. What two ideas conveyed in 1 Kings 1:5-6 indicate the lifestyle of David's son Adonijah? How may Adonijah's lifestyle have affected his actions in 1 Kings 1:7–10, 25–26? _____

_____

_____

_____

b. What personal insights can you draw from these passages? _____

_____

3. What key people in David's government was Adonijah able to get to help him (1 Kings 1:7)? Who remained faithful to David (1 Kings 1:8)? _____

_____

_____

4. a. As David begins to approach the difficult issue Nathan the prophet presents to him, of what important fact is David reminded (1 Kings 1:29)? _____

b. How did this truth encourage David as well as those to whom he spoke? _____

_____

c. Apply this principle to your own life. _____

_____

5. a. Carefully study 1 Kings 1:10–48 to determine how Adonijah was stopped. Record your observations here. _____

_____

_____

_____

b. What can you learn about God from this event? Where possible, support your conclusions from the passage, listing the specific verses. _____

_____

_____

6. What were some of the end results in the lives of the people who chose not to do things God's way (1 Kings 1:49–53)? _____

_____

_____

DISCOVERY 2/David's charge to his son

7. a. What is David's greatest concern in his final charge to Solomon (1 Kings 2:1–4)? _____

_____

_____

b. What does this concern indicate about David's heart attitude toward God and that which is important to God?

_____

c. If you have a child, what is your greatest concern for him or her? What specifically are you doing about it? _____

_____

_____

8. a. What great project was Solomon called to do? Who called him to the task (1 Chron. 22:6–11)? _____

_____

b. What did David know about his son Solomon (1 Chron. 22:5)? _____

_____

c. Carefully study 1 Chronicles 22:5–17 and determine at least five ways in which David prepared Solomon for the future, particularly in regard to Solomon's special calling.

_____

_____

_____

_____

_____

d. What principles did David say would secure true prosperity for his son (1 Chron. 22:12–13)? Think of at least one practical way in which you can convey this same truth to your child. _____

_____

_____

_____

9. a. According to 1 Chronicles 22:12, what are two qualities David desired his son to have? How did David feel Solomon would acquire these qualities? _____

_____

b. David's statements must have affected Solomon. What did Solomon ask of the Lord in 1 Kings 3:7–10? _____

_____

c. How did the Lord respond to Solomon's request (1 Kings 3:10–14)? _____

_____

_____

d. Why is Solomon's request an important one for us to consider for our lives? Have you ever personally made this request to the Lord? If not, why not stop and do so now. _____

_____

_____

10. a. Though Solomon was to take the lead in the great task the Lord had set before him, who would help him (1 Chron. 22:17–19)? _____

_____

_____

b. What key statement does David make in 1 Chronicles 22:18 that would be of great encouragement to a leader of Israel? What did the Lord do to make it possible for time to be given to the work? _____

_____

_____

c. What heart attitude was to accompany the labor (1 Chron. 22:19)? _____

_____

_____

d. How can you apply this to your life? _____

_____

_____

DISCOVERY 3/David's address about the temple
Read 1 Chronicles 28.

11. Who drew up the plans for the majestic Solomonic temple? What does this public address reveal to you about David? About God? _____

_____

_____

_____

_____

DISCOVERY 4/Sacrificial offering for the temple

Read 1 Chronicles 29.

12. What was particularly important about the offerings that were made for the temple (1 Chron. 29:1–9, 14–17)?

_____

_____

DISCOVERY 5/David's final prayer

13. In 1 Chronicles 29:10–19 we read the last public prayer of one who walked with God. What do you learn about prayer from David ? _____

_____

_____

_____

14. Using David's prayer as a source, develop at least five principles about how we should live. _____

_____

_____

_____

_____

_____

Key Principles from Lesson 13

1. Remembering the powerful works of God in our lives encourages us in present difficulties (1 Kings 1:29).

2. The purposes of God cannot be thwarted (1 Kings and 1 Chron. 22:9–10).

3. Walking in God's ways brings godly success (1 Kings 2:3 and 1 Chron. 22:13).

4. It is God who commissions us to do tasks for Him (1 Chron. 22:10).

5. It is wise to set our heart and soul to seek the Lord in any leadership role (1 Chron. 22:19).

6. It is pleasing to the Lord when we ask Him for the ability to discern between good and evil (1 Kings 3:9–10).

7. Willingly offering back to God with a whole heart that which He has given us brings joy (1 Chron. 29:9, 14).